HOW DO THEY MAKE THAT?

BREAD

Jody Jensen Shaffer and John Willis

www.av2books.com

AV² provides enriched content that supplements and complements this book. Weigl's AV² books strive to create inspired learning and engage young minds in a total learning experience.

Your AV² Media Enhanced books come alive with...

Audio
Listen to sections of the book read aloud.

Key Words
Study vocabulary, and complete a matching word activity.

Video
Watch informative video clips.

Quizzes
Test your knowledge.

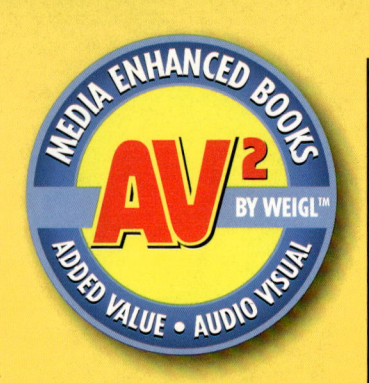

Go to www.av2books.com, and enter this book's unique code.

BOOK CODE
U229782

Embedded Weblinks
Gain additional information for research.

Slide Show
View images and captions, and prepare a presentation.

AV² by Weigl brings you media enhanced books that support active learning.

Try This!
Complete activities and hands-on experiments.

... and much, much more!

Published by AV² by Weigl
350 5th Avenue, 59th Floor
New York, NY 10118
Website: www.av2books.com

Copyright © 2017 AV² by Weigl
All rights reserved. No part of this publication may be reproduced, stored in a retrieval system, or transmitted in any form or by any means, electronic, mechanical, photocopying, recording, or otherwise, without the prior written permission of the publisher.

Library of Congress Cataloging-in-Publication Data

Names: Shaffer, Jody Jensen, author | and Willis, John, author.
Title: Bread / Jody Jensen Shaffer.
Description: New York : AV2 by Weigl, [2017] | Series: How do they make that?
 | Includes index.
Identifiers: LCCN 2016005645 (print) | LCCN 2016006981 (ebook) | ISBN
 9781489645296 (hard cover : alk. paper) | ISBN 9781489649973 (soft cover :
 alk. paper) | ISBN 9781489645302 (Multi-user ebk.)
Subjects: LCSH: Bread--Juvenile literature. | Baked products
 industry--Juvenile literature.
Classification: LCC TX769 .S3332 2017 (print) | LCC TX769 (ebook) | DDC
 641.815--dc23
LC record available at http://lccn.loc.gov/2016005645

Printed in the United States of America in Brainerd, Minnesota
1 2 3 4 5 6 7 8 9 0 20 19 18 17 16

072016
210716

Project Coordinator: John Willis   Art Director: Terry Paulhus

Every reasonable effort has been made to trace ownership and to obtain permission to reprint copyright material. The publishers would be pleased to have any errors or omissions brought to their attention so that they may be corrected in subsequent printings.

Weigl acknowledges Getty Images, iStock, Dreamstime, Newscom, Shutterstock, and Alamy as its primary image suppliers for this title.

Contents

AV² Book Code	2
Hearty Bread	4
Grain	6
On a Farm	8
To the Flour Mill	12
At the Bakery	20
Onto Your Plate	28
Quiz	30
Key Words/Index	31
Log on to www.av2books.com	32

Hearty Bread

What is chewy and delicious? Bread. It is great for turkey sandwiches and sweet French toast. Many meals include some kind of bread. There are many different kinds of bread as well. Sourdough is tangy. White bread is soft. Whole wheat is chewy. What kind of bread do you like?

Have you thought about how bread is made? There are many steps. The first step starts on a farm. That is where grain is grown. Bread is made from grain. Grain comes from plants grown in large fields.

Bread is commonly eaten during meals such as breakfast, lunch, and dinner.

Bread 5

There are three main kinds of wheat: hard wheat, durum wheat, and soft wheat.

Grain

Wheat is the grain used to make most bread. Wheat kernels can be red, brown, purple, blue, or white. Some wheat is planted in the winter. Some is planted in the spring.

Some wheat is hard and contains lots of protein. The protein is very important. It makes bread dough strong and **elastic**. Flour mills want to know how much protein is in wheat. They pay different prices for more protein.

All grains have three parts. **Bran** is the hard outer layer of the grain. The **germ** is the part of the grain that sprouts. The **endosperm** is the soft inside of the grain.

Soft wheats are used to make cookies and crackers. Durum wheat is used to make pasta. Hard wheats are used to make bread and other products that rise when baked.

On a Farm

A farmer plants wheat seeds in the fall or spring. It depends on the kind of wheat that is grown. The wheat is planted with a drill. The drill is pulled by a tractor. The drill makes long, narrow **trenches** in the ground. Then, it drops seeds in the trenches.

Wheat plants look like yard grass at first. Then, they grow heads. This is the part with many seeds at the top. The plant turns green and then gold. It dries and hardens when the wheat is ripe. Then, it is ready to harvest. Farmers use a **combine** to do this. Combines can harvest an acre (0.4 hectares) of wheat in six minutes or less.

Hard winter wheat is grown in Kansas, Oklahoma, and Texas. Hard spring wheat is grown in Washington, Montana, North Dakota, and South Dakota.

A lot of wheat is needed to make all the different kinds of bread eaten today.

Bread 9

The combine turns and pushes the heads of the wheat plants. They go against a long, curved blade called a sickle. The sickle cuts the heads off the plants. The combine shakes and beats the wheat seeds from the heads. It also separates the heads from the chaff. This is the outside of the seed.

In the summer, you can hear the wheat in a field crack in the heat. Water inside the wheat kernel heats up. It cracks open the chaff and makes a noise.

Using a combine can make the process of harvesting much faster.

Bread 11

The chaff is discarded after being removed from the wheat.

To the Flour Mill

After the grain is harvested, the farmer loads it onto a truck. Next, the grain goes to a flour mill. A flour mill cleans, separates, and grinds the grain into flour. Flour is important. It is one of the three main ingredients in bread.

Wheat is cleaned in several ways. Air machines blow on the grain to remove dirt and the stalk. This is called winnowing. The chaff is also separated from the wheat.

The tables are used to make sure rocks, sticks, and other debris do not go into the flour.

14   How Do They Make That?

The wheat is shaken on special tables. Magnets remove bits of metal that may be in the grain.

Different kinds of wheat have different amounts of protein. The mill mixes wheat to make different flour batches. Some batches have more protein. Some batches have less. After the batches are mixed, the wheat is cleaned again.

More machines are used to clean the grain. A scourer cleans the mud off the wheat kernel. It also breaks up damaged wheat. Other machines take off the skin of the wheat and remove the beard. The beard is the hairy piece at the top of the grain.

Because it is very finely ground, flour is soft and powdery.

Now, the clean wheat can be ground into different kinds of flour. The wheat goes through a series of metal rollers. The rollers grind the grain.

To make white bread, the parts of the grain are separated. The grain moves through a series of **sieves** and machines. The machines are called break rolls. The endosperm is sorted from the bran. The grain cannot be cracked or crushed. That will make the flour look brown, not white.

Some flour is packed into large sacks to be transported to bakeries.

To make whole wheat bread, the outer skin is ground into flour. One hundred percent whole wheat bread is often hard. Bakers can add wheat **gluten** to whole wheat flour. Gluten makes whole wheat bread softer. It helps make bread dough rise.

The clean, separated flour is then stored in large silos. Workers take samples of the grain and flour. They test the flour to make sure it is good. Some factories spray the flour with **chemicals**. This keeps out insects and insect eggs. Some flour may be loaded into tanker trucks. Now it is ready for the bakery.

At the Bakery

A bakery turns flour into bread dough by adding water and yeast. Yeast is a tiny, living **organism** that helps make bread rise. Protein found in hard wheat also helps bread rise. Bakers test the flour. They make sure it will rise and produce loaves that are the same size.

Mixing is done in large bowls with metal beaters. Mixers can mix up to 2,000 pounds (907 kilograms) of dough per minute. It takes about 12 minutes to mix a large batch of dough. Then, the dough is left to rise for about eight minutes. The yeast and proteins in the dough form and trap **gas bubbles**. The bubbles make the dough rise. The more the dough rises, the softer the bread will be.

Bread dough is very sticky. Large mixing bowls are used to make sure all the ingredients are spread evenly.

The molding machine is the next step for the dough. It is used to shape the dough. The machine separates the dough into big round balls for sandwich bread. Short round balls are made for hamburger and hotdog buns. The pieces are placed in pans for baking.

Different amounts of dough and different shapes of dough are needed to make different types of bread.

Bread 23

Next, the dough is left to rise a second time. The baker places the dough in a warm, moist cupboard called a prover for 30 minutes. From the prover, a **conveyor belt** moves the dough through a tunnel oven to be baked. The bread bakes for 25 to 30 minutes. Large bakeries can make thousands of loaves of bread each day.

When the bread is finished baking, it is put onto racks to cool. Finished bread smells great. It is golden brown and crusty on the top and sides. The middle is soft and chewy.

Each American eats about 53 pounds (24 kg) of bread per year.

Bread loaves need to cool for about 30 minutes after being baked.

Bread 25

Once the bread cools, it is sliced. A slicing maching cuts even slices. The blades must be kept very sharp. They are changed every two weeks.

The sliced bread is packaged in plastic bags. At some bakeries, workers tie the bags closed by hand. Other bakeries use a machine that seals the bags shut with heat. Then, the loaves are stored in crates so they will not be crushed.

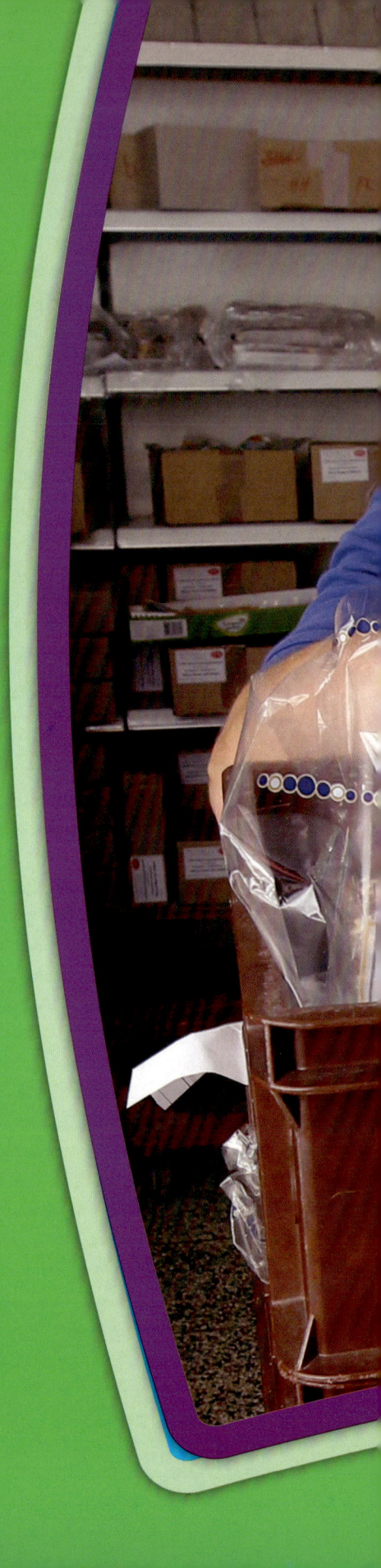

The sliced bread may be put into bags that look just like the ones at the grocery store.

Bread 27

Once the bread is put into bags it travels to the grocery store, where it is put on display to be sold.

Onto Your Plate

The bread is loaded onto trucks and delivered to stores as quickly as possible. People like to eat fresh bread. Fresh bread is soft and delicious. Older bread becomes stale. It can be hard and dry. The fresh bread goes to the grocery aisle. There you can find many kinds to choose from.

What will you make with bread? Try a gooey grilled cheese sandwich for lunch. Buttery toast is good. You can have a sweet piece of cinnamon raisin bread with jam. Any way you try it, bread is delicious.

Quiz

Match the steps with the pictures.

A. Harvest grain
B. Grind flour
C. Dough is mixed
D. Baked in ovens
E. Sliced and bagged
F. Sent to grocery store

Answers
1. B 2. D 3. C 4. A 5. E 6. F

30   How Do They Make That?

Key Words

bran: the outer coat of cereal grain seeds

chemicals: substances made using chemistry

combine: a large machine used by farmers to gather and clean crops from a field

conveyor belt: a moving belt that takes materials from one place to another in a factory

elastic: to be able to stretch

endosperm: nutritive tissue found in plant seeds

gas bubbles: tiny balls of gas trapped in bread dough

germ: the embryo of a cereal seed

gluten: a mixture of proteins that makes bread dough elastic

organism: a living plant or animal

sieves: containers with many holes used to separate large pieces from small pieces

trenches: long, narrow holes

Index

bakery 19, 20
bran 7, 17

chaff 10, 12, 13
combine 8, 10, 11

durum wheat 6, 7

endosperm 7, 17

farm 4, 8, 13
flour 7, 13, 14, 15, 16, 17, 18, 19, 20, 30
flour mill 7, 13, 15

germ 7
gluten 19
grain 4, 7, 13, 15, 17, 19, 30

hard wheat 6, 7, 8, 20

protein 7, 15, 20

soft wheat 6, 7

white bread 4, 17
whole wheat bread 4, 19

yeast 20

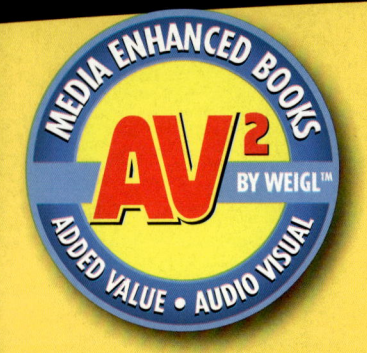

Log on to www.av2books.com

AV² by Weigl brings you media enhanced books that support active learning. Go to www.av2books.com, and enter the special code found on page 2 of this book. You will gain access to enriched and enhanced content that supplements and complements this book. Content includes video, audio, weblinks, quizzes, a slide show, and activities.

AV² Online Navigation

Book Pages
AV² pages directly correspond to pages in the book.

Audio
Listen to sections of the book read aloud.

Video
Watch informative video clips.

Key Words
Study vocabulary, and complete a matching word activity.

Embedded Weblinks
Gain additional information for research.

Quizzes
Test your knowledge.

Slide Show
View images and captions, and prepare a presentation.

Try This!
Complete activities and hands-on experiments.

AV² was built to bridge the gap between print and digital. We encourage you to tell us what you like and what you want to see in the future.

Sign up to be an AV² Ambassador at www.av2books.com/ambassador.

Due to the dynamic nature of the Internet, some of the URLs and activities provided as part of AV² by Weigl may have changed or ceased to exist. AV² by Weigl accepts no responsibility for any such changes. All media enhanced books are regularly monitored to update addresses and sites in a timely manner. Contact AV² by Weigl at 1-866-649-3445 or av2books@weigl.com with any questions, comments, or feedback.

32   How Do They Make That?